Contents

4 Life at Sea

6 Relaxing

8 Grooming

10 Swimming

12 Diving

14 Eating

18 Caring

20 Sleeping

22 Glossary

23 Index

24 A Note to Parents

Life at Sea

These are sea otters.
They spend most of
their lives in the water.

Sea Otters

Series Editor Deborah Lock
Editor Arpita Nath
Senior Art Editor Ann Cannings
Project Art Editor Tanvi Nathyal
Picture Researcher Sumedha Chopra
Production Editors Christine Ni
Senior Producer, Pre-production Nikoleta Parasaki
DTP Designers Vijay Kandwal, Dheeraj Singh
Jacket Designer Charlotte Jennings
Managing Editor Soma B. Chowdhury
Managing Art Editor Ahlawat Gunjan
Art Director Martin Wilson

Reading Consultant
Linda Gambrell, Ph.D.

First published in Great Britain in 2016
by Dorling Kindersley Limited
80 Strand, London, WC2R 0RL

A CIP catalogue record for this book
is available from the British Library
ISBN: 978-0-2412-2512-7

Printed and bound in China.
The publisher would like to thank Jim Curland and Frank Reynolds from Friends of the Sea Otter (www.seaotters.org) for their advice.
The publisher would also like to thank the following for their kind permission to reproduce their photographs:
(Key: a=above, b=below/bottom, c=centre, l=left, r=right, t=top)
1 Alamy Images: Harry Walker / Design Pics Inc. **3 iStockphoto.com:** RobsonAbbott (br). **4-5 naturepl.com:** Bertie Gregor (b). **5 Dreamstime.com:** Nilanjan Bhattacharya (cr, br). **iStockphoto.com:** RobsonAbbott (tc). **6 Getty Images:** Stuart Westmorland / The Image Bank (c). **6-7 Getty Images:** David Gomez / E+. **8-9 Corbis:** Frans Lanting (b). **9 Getty Images:** Cameron Rutt / Moment (tl). **10-11 Getty Images:** Ai Angel Gentel / Moment Open. **12 123RF.com:** Kevin Griffin (bl). **13 naturepl.com:** Doc White. **14-15 Getty Images:** Jeff Foott. **16 Science Photo Library:** Thomas & Pat Leeson (b). **17 Corbis:** Hal Beral. **18-19 Corbis:** Steven Kazlowski / Science Faction (b). **19 Getty Images:** Donald M. Jones / Minden Pictures (tr). **20-21 naturepl.com:** Tom Mangelsen. **22 123RF.com:** Kevin Griffin (cla). **Corbis:** Brandon D. Cole (clb); Tim Fitzharris / Minden Pictures (bl). **Dreamstime.com:** Nilanjan Bhattacharya (tl). **24 Dreamstime.com:** Nilanjan Bhattacharya (br). **Endpapers: Dreamstime.com:** Kristen Wahlquist / Xfkirsten. **Jacket credits:** Front: **Corbis:** Kevin Schafe (c). **Dreamstime.com:** Kirsten Wahlquist / Xfkirsten (tc) Back: **naturepl.com:** Bertie Gregory t

All other images © Dorling Kindersley
For further information see: www.dkimages.com

Relaxing

They can float on their backs.

Grooming

Their fur keeps them
warm and dry.
They brush their fur
and roll over
to keep clean.

whiskers

fur

9

Swimming

Sea otters use
their webbed feet
and flat tails to swim.

flat tail   webbed foot

Diving

They swim around
to find food.
They dive in and
out of the kelp.

kelp

Eating

They have strong teeth to bite into their food.

crab

teeth

They can hit a stone
on a shellfish to crack
the shell open.

Caring

Otter pups can only float to begin with. Their mums take care of them.

Sleeping

Sea otters may wrap kelp around their bodies when they sleep.

kelp

Glossary

Fur
soft hair covering the skin of some animals

Kelp
large seaweed with a long stalk

Shellfish
sea animal that has a shell

Webbed
fingers or toes joined with a piece of skin

Whiskers
long hair growing on the face of some animals

Index

care 18

clean 8

crab 14

dive 12

float 6, 18

food 14

fur 8, 9

kelp 12, 20

pups 18

roll 8

shellfish 16

sleep 20

stone 16

swim 10, 12

tail 10, 11

teeth 14, 15

webbed feet 10, 11

whiskers 8

A Note to Parents

DK Readers is a four-level interactive reading adventure series for children, developing the habit of reading widely for both pleasure and information.

Beautiful illustrations and superb full-colour photographs combine with engaging, easy-to-read narratives to offer a fresh approach to each subject in the series. Each DK Reader is guaranteed to capture a child's interest while developing his or her reading skills, general knowledge and love of reading.

The four levels of DK Readers are aimed at different reading abilities, enabling you to choose the books that are exactly right for your child:

Level 1: Learning to read
Level 2: Beginning to read
Level 3: Beginning to read alone
Level 4: Reading alone

The "normal" age at which a child begins to read can be anywhere from three to eight years old. Adult participation through the lower levels is very helpful for providing encouragement, discussing storylines and sounding out unfamiliar words.

No matter which level you select, you can be sure that you are helping your child learn to read, then read to learn!